KABOOM!

WILE E. COYOTE EXPERIMENTS WITH
CHEMICAL REACTIONS

by MARK WEAKLAND   illustrated by LOIC BILLIAU

Published in 2017 by Capstone Press
A Capstone Imprint
1710 Roe Crest Drive
North Mankato, Minnesota 56003
www.mycapstone.com

Library of Congress Cataloging-in-Publication Data
Names: Weakland, Mark, author. | Billiau, Loic, illustrator.
Title: Kaboom! : Wile E. Coyote experiments with chemical reactions / by Mark Weakland ;
illustrated by Loic Billiau.
Description: North Mankato, Minnesota : Capstone Press, 2017. | Series:
Warner Brothers. Wile E. Coyote, physical science genus | Includes bibliographical references
and index.
Identifiers: LCCN 2016045596| ISBN 9781515737339 (library binding) |
ISBN 9781515737377 (pbk.) | ISBN 9781515737490 (ebook (pdf))
Subjects: LCSH: Chemical reactions—Experiments—Juvenile literature. | Reactivity
(Chemistry)—Experiments—Juvenile literature. | Wile E. Coyote (Fictitious character)—Juvenile
literature. | CYAC: Chemistry—Experiments.
Classification: LCC QD501 .W4788 2017 | DDC 541/.39—dc23
LC record available at https://lccn.loc.gov/2016045596

Editorial Credits
Michelle Hasselius, editor; Ashlee Suker, designer; Steve Walker, production specialist

Capstone Press thanks Paul Ohmann, PhD, Associate Professor of Physics at
the University of St. Thomas for his help creating this book.

Printed and bound in the USA.
010057S17CG

TABLE OF CONTENTS

React!

Being a genius is a tough job. For all his brainpower, Wile E. Coyote can never get rid of that Road Runner. Maybe it's because Wile E. doesn't understand the science behind all of his tricks.

Coyote
(Hungrius carnivorii)

Road Runner
(Speedius birdius)

Take **chemical reactions**, for example. Wile E. is trying to use chemistry to defeat Road Runner. He wants to create a gas that will lift the balloon. The rising balloon will strike a match and fire a rocket. BOOM! Road Runner will be toast.

But Wile E.'s plan is doomed to fail. If he knew more about chemical reactions, he'd know why his machine isn't working. And he could make one that worked.

chemical reaction—a process in which one or more substances are made into a new substance or substances

Wile E. is surrounded by chemical reactions. They cause his bread to rise. They make his cleansers work. They digest the food in his belly. Every time Wile E. lights a fire or browns meat in a skillet, he starts a chemical reaction.

Kitchen Classics
R R STEW
4 c. of water
1 tsp. of salt
1 FROZEN ROAD RUNNER
2 POTATOES

ACME KIT

Not everything is a chemical reaction. A piece of
bread turning to toast is a reaction. But a giant pot
of water growing hotter and hotter is not. Wile E.
is hoping to freeze Road Runner for his stew.
Would that be a chemical reaction? Let's find out.

CHAPTER 1

THE ELEMENTS OF MATTER

Everything Is Matter

Wile E. needs one frozen Road Runner to make his stew. And he needs to understand **matter** to make his chemical reactions work. Unfortunately, Wile E. is having trouble getting either one!

Everything is made of matter, including water, soup, and coyotes. Matter exists in one of three forms: solid, liquid, or gas. When solid ice melts, its form changes to liquid. When water boils into steam, its form changes to gas. But these changes are not chemical reactions. Water is still water, even when it changes form. Chemical reactions occur only when substances are changed into entirely new substances.

Speaking of reactions, look at Road Runner.
He thinks this change is hilarious!

matter—particles of which everything
in the universe is made

Wile E. knows all about winter. He knows that salt melts snow and ice. But does he know that snow, ice, and salt are made of **atoms**?

Matter's basic building blocks are tiny things called atoms. There are more than 100 different kinds of atoms. Each kind is called an **element**. Elements are often organized in the Periodic Table of Elements.

When atoms stick together, it's called bonding. Atoms bond because they are attracted to one another. When one atom bonds to another, a **molecule** is formed.

atom—a tiny particle of which everything is made

element—a basic substance that is made up of only one kind of atom

molecule—the atoms making up the smallest unit of a substance; H_2O is a molecule of water

A **compound** is a substance that forms when different kinds of atoms bond together. For example, salt is not made from salt atoms. Salt is made from one atom of sodium and one atom of chlorine. Sodium and chlorine are elements. When the atoms of these elements bond, they form a new substance—salt! Salt's chemical name is sodium chloride, or NaCl.

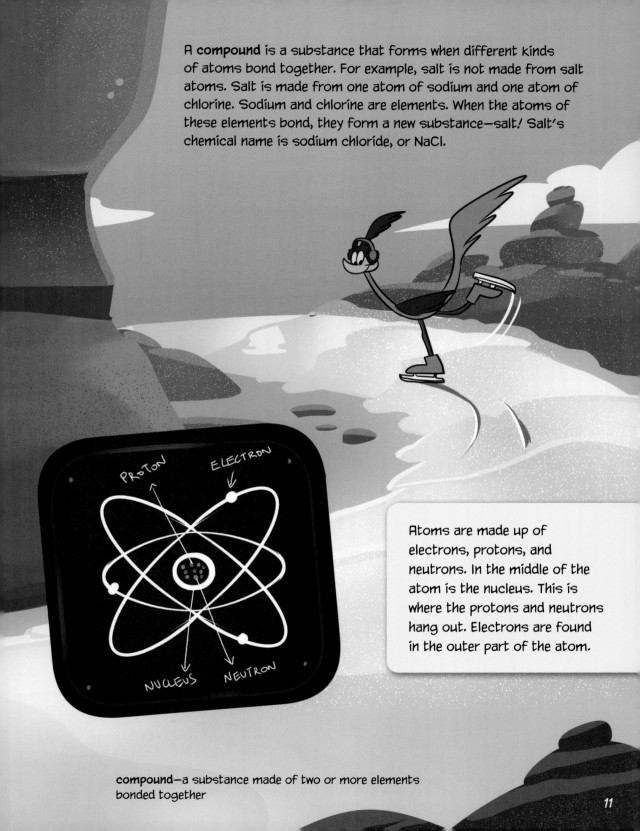

PROTON

ELECTRON

NUCLEUS

NEUTRON

Atoms are made up of electrons, protons, and neutrons. In the middle of the atom is the nucleus. This is where the protons and neutrons hang out. Electrons are found in the outer part of the atom.

compound—a substance made of two or more elements bonded together

CHAPTER 2

CHEMISTRY SET

Reagents and Products

Wile E. hopes to use vinegar and baking soda to blow up Road Runner. Will his plan work? Let's learn more about his chemical reaction and find out.

Reagents are the substances used to make chemical reactions. In Wile E.'s plan, vinegar is one reagent. Baking soda is another. Reagents come together and react to make a new substance, or **product**. Wile E.'s two reagents will come together and make carbon dioxide gas, or CO_2. CO_2 is a compound formed when one atom of carbon bonds with two atoms of oxygen.

MAKE A DESERT SNOWBALL!

NEW PLAN

BAKING SODA

VINEGAR

KABOOM

CO_2

reagent—a substance that takes part in and undergoes change during a reaction

product—something that is made

Wile E. thinks this CO_2 gas will erupt into a giant explosion. Could this finally be the end of Road Runner?

ACME
BAKING SODA

ACME VINEGAR

Reaction Rate

Wile is learning that not all chemical reactions occur at the same rate. Some reactions happen quickly, such as an explosion. Others take a long time, such as metal rusting. Reagents turn into products at a certain speed. This speed is called the **reaction rate**.

When energy is added to a reaction, the reaction rate changes. The added energy could be from heat, sunlight, or electricity.

HERE!

MAKE A DESERT SNOWBALL!

FUN!

PFFT

ACME BAKING SODA

ACME VINEG

reaction rate—how fast or slow a reaction takes place

The reaction rate also changes when more or less of the reagents are used. This is why Wile E.'s first plan fizzled out. He only added a little vinegar to the baking soda. That only made a little carbon dioxide.

Wile E.'s second plan blew up in his face. Why? He added too much vinegar. The baking soda dissolved quickly, so the reagents reacted quickly.

CHAPTER 3

LIGHTS, CAMERAS, REACTION!

Activation Energy

There are many types of chemical reactions. One type combines two substances to make a third substance.

Wile E. wants to use water to wash away Road Runner. Too bad he's out of water. But Wile E. has a plan—he'll make his own! Wile E. knows water is a compound made from one oxygen molecule and two hydrogen molecules. But simply mixing hydrogen and oxygen molecules together won't work. Why? Not all substances react when you put them together. Putting hydrogen with oxygen just makes a big cloud of these gases.

Often, adding energy gets a reaction going. This is called **activation energy.** In his second try, Wile E. added energy by striking a match. What a dangerous thing to do! Hydrogen gas catches fire in the blink of an eye. And oxygen makes things burn fast. Hydrogen and oxygen atoms make water molecules when energy is added. But the water is created through an explosion.

activation energy—the least amount of energy required to activate atoms or molecules to a state in which they can undergo a chemical reaction

Iron Oxide

Wile E. has a towering plan for catching Road Runner. But a chemical reaction is about to spoil it. Poor Wile E.!

Rusting is another type of chemical reaction. When iron comes in contact with oxygen in the presence of water, iron oxide forms. This is also called rust.

Wile E. has already learned that reaction rates can speed up or slow down. But he didn't learn his lesson very well. He hasn't noticed that the iron tower is rusting quickly. Paint and oil keep iron from coming in contact with oxygen in the air. But the legs of the tower have no paint or oil on them. Iron oxide also forms more quickly in wet places. Two of the tower legs are planted in marshy soil!

Next time Wile E. should think more carefully about reaction rates. But right now he's only thinking about the ground!

Combustion

Burning is another chemical reaction. Right now Wile E. is burning gasoline in the engine of his race car.

Burning is called **combustion**. It is a reaction that produces energy in the form of heat. Combustion occurs when oxygen combines with fuel. There are many types of fuel. In a campfire, wood is the fuel. In a candle flame, wax is the fuel. And in Wile E.'s race car, gasoline is the fuel.

When a fuel and oxygen react, two products are created—water and carbon dioxide. Fuel such as oil and coal are "dirty." They produce other products as well, such as soot.

Combustion reactions make trucks, cars, trains, and airplanes go. These reactions occur when energy is added to oxygen and fuel. In an engine, spark plugs provide energy. It doesn't take much, just one little spark. But without a spark, Wile E. isn't going anywhere!

SPARK PLUGS

BUMP BUMP

combustion—burning; a fast chemical change that occurs when oxygen combines with another substance

Combustion and Oxidizers

Wile E. loves rockets even more than race cars. Look at him go!

Like cars, rockets are propelled by a combustion reaction. The combustion requires fuel and a source of oxygen. In rockets, the fuel is often liquid hydrogen. The source of oxygen is called the **oxidizer**. In a rocket, the oxidizer is liquid oxygen.

oxidizer—a chemical that a fuel requires to burn

Some type of heat starts the combustion. For his rocket, Wile E. uses a lit fuse. Heat starts combustion, but heat is also a product of combustion. In other words, burning begins with heat. The burning also produces heat. The produced heat creates even more burning.

This cycle of heat, burning, and more heat is why combustion reactions happen very quickly. After combustion starts, additional heat is not needed to keep it going. As Wile E. is finding out, combustion is like a wildfire. Once it starts, it is difficult to stop!

BLAM!

CHAPTER 4

REACTIONS INSIDE AND OUT

Catalyst

To catch Road Runner, Wile E. needs more than fancy shoes. He needs chemical reactions. Lots of them!

Inside his body, millions of chemical reactions are happening every minute. They happen in his lungs and in his muscles. They even happen in his brain. Without chemical reactions, Wile E. couldn't even think about catching Road Runner.

Chemical reactions outside of the body often need high heat to get started. Think of a match lighting a fire. But reactions inside the body start without a match. And they operate at low temperatures.

ROAD RUNNERS 13

acme RUNNING

Chemical reactions inside Wile E.'s body use **catalysts**. Catalysts are substances that lower the amount of energy needed for reactions to start. They also speed up reactions, even at low temperatures.

The catalysts inside Wile E. are called **enzymes**. They help protect his body from harmful temperatures. And enzymes let reactions occur at Wile E.'s body temperature, which is 100 degrees Fahrenheit (38 degrees Celsius). There's no need to sweat it when catalysts are on your side.

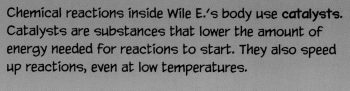

FOOSH !

catalyst—a substance that speeds up a chemical reaction without being used up by the chemical reaction

enzyme—a special protein that speeds up chemical reactions in the body

Explosion

What's one of Wile E.'s favorite plans for getting rid of his enemy? A stick of dynamite and a giant explosion! But if he isn't careful, he'll only blow up himself.

Wile E.'s stick of dynamite is a solid chemical fuel. A burning fuse provides the heat energy to start the reaction. During an explosion, reacting materials create gases. These gases create pressure around the reaction. The added energy from the pressure causes the chemical reaction to go very quickly. The total reaction time can be a millionth of a second or less.

WOOSH!

During an explosion a shock wave rushes out at **supersonic** speed. This wave can cause a lot of damage. Explosions knock down walls, blow craters in the earth, and launch coyotes into the air. What has four legs, fur, and flies? A coyote, of course!

The shock wave from an explosion can travel as fast as 22,000 miles (35,406 kilometers) per hour. Temperatures in an explosion reach more than 9,000 degrees F (4,982 degrees C).

KABOOM!!

supersonic—faster than the speed of sound

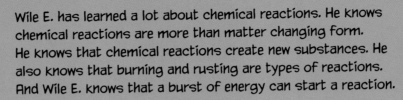

Wile E. has learned a lot about chemical reactions. He knows chemical reactions are more than matter changing form. He knows that chemical reactions create new substances. He also knows that burning and rusting are types of reactions. And Wile E. knows that a burst of energy can start a reaction.

At the beginning, a lack of energy is why Wile E.'s machine didn't work. It needed a spark. But in the end, poor Wile E. has forgotten the most important thing. He forgot that in a chemical reaction, a spark can lead to an explosion.

GLOSSARY

activation energy (AK-tuh-vay-shun en-uhr-JEE)—the least amount of energy required to activate atoms or molecules to a state in which they undergo a chemical reaction

atom (AT-uhm)—a tiny particle of which everything is made

catalyst (CAT-uh-list)—a substance that speeds up a chemical reaction without being used up by the chemical reaction

chemical reaction (KE-muh-kuhl ree-AK-shuhn)—a process in which one or more substances are made into a new substance or substances

combustion (kuhm-BUS-chuhn)—burning; a fast chemical change that occurs when oxygen combines with another substance

compound (KAHM-paund)—a substance made of two or more elements bonded together

element (EL-uh-muhnt)—a basic substance that is made up of only one kind of atom

enzyme (EN-zime)—a special protein that speeds up chemical reactions in the body

matter (MAT-ur)—particles of which everything in the universe is made

molecule (MOL-uh-kyool)—the atoms making up the smallest unit of a substance; H_2O is a molecule of water

oxidizer (OK-suh-dize-ur)—a chemical that a fuel requires to burn

product (PROD-uhkt)—something that is made

reaction rate (ree-AK-shuhn RAYT)—how fast or slow a reaction takes place

reagent (ree-AY-juhnt)—a substance that takes part in and undergoes change during a reaction

supersonic (soo-pur-SON-ik)—faster than the speed of sound

30

READ MORE

Biskup, Agnieszka. *Super Cool Chemical Reaction Activities with Max Axiom.* Max Axiom Science and Engineering Activities. North Mankato, Minn.: Capstone Press, 2015.

Maurer, Tracy. *Changing Matter: Understanding Physical and Chemical Changes.* My Science Library. Vero Beach, Fla.: Rourke Educational Media, 2013.

Navarro, Paula, and Ángels Jiménez. *Incredible Experiments with Chemical Reactions and Mixtures.* Magic Science. Hauppauge, New York: Barron's Educational Series, 2014.

INTERNET SITES

FactHound offers a safe, fun way to find Internet sites related to this book. All of the sites on FactHound have been researched by our staff.

Here's all you do:

Visit *www.facthound.com*

Type in this code: 9781515737339

Check out projects, games and lots more at
www.capstonekids.com

Super-cool stuff!

INDEX

OTHER BOOKS IN THIS SERIES

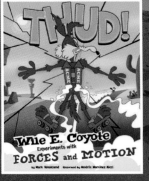

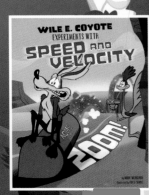